George Ricker Berry

The Letters of the Rm 2 Collection

In the British Museum, with Transliteraion, Notes and Glossary

George Ricker Berry

The Letters of the Rm 2 Collection
In the British Museum, with Transliteraion, Notes and Glossary

ISBN/EAN: 9783337019105

Printed in Europe, USA, Canada, Australia, Japan

Cover: Foto ©Andreas Hilbeck / pixelio.de

More available books at **www.hansebooks.com**

THE LETTERS

OF THE

R^M 2 COLLECTION

IN THE

BRITISH MUSEUM, WITH TRANSLITERATION, NOTES
AND GLOSSARY

BY

GEORGE RICKER BERRY
THE UNIVERSITY OF CHICAGO

CHICAGO
The University of Chicago Press
1896

A DISSERTATION PRESENTED TO THE FACULTY OF THE GRADUATE SCHOOL ARTS AND LITERATURE OF THE UNIVERSITY OF CHICAGO, IN CANDIDACY FOR THE DEGREE OF DOCTOR OF PHILOSOPHY.

[Reprinted from HEBRAICA, Vol. XI., Nos. 3 and 4. Chicago, Ill.]

THE LETTERS OF THE R^M 2. COLLECTION (ZA VIII. pp. 341-359).

By George Ricker Berry.

The University of Chicago.

The term *Assyrian Letters* may for convenience be applied to Letters written either in Assyrian or Babylonian. A distinction is usually made between Letters in the proper sense and the Reports of government officials, which are generally formal and conventional. No clear distinction, however, is possible. Many tablets, properly called Letters, are, in reality, Reports from officials to the king. Such Letter-reports are much less interesting than the more informal—or rather less official—Letters.

In this introduction I aim to give a résumé of the work done upon Assyrian Letters. In some cases, it has not been considered necessary to attempt a distinction between Letters, Letter-reports and Reports.

In the narrow sense in which it is ordinarily used, the term Assyrian Letters designates a large mass of literature which is, by common consent, referred to the period of the Sargon dynasty. In a wider sense, however, it should also include the Letters found at Tel el-Amarna in 1887. The latter belong to the XVth century B. C., and are now in the museums at London, Berlin and Gizeh, with the exception of a few in the possession of private parties. The following is the most important literature on the Tel el-Amarna tablets: (1) *Der Thontafelfund von El Amarna*, Hugo Winckler, Berlin, 1890, containing the cuneiform text of 240 Letters, besides six other tablets which are not Letters. A large part of these tablets is now in Berlin, some are in Gizeh, and a few in the possession of M. Golenischeff of St. Petersburg. (2) *The Tell el-Amarna Tablets in the British Museum with Autotype Facsimiles*, C. Bezold and E. A. W. Budge, London, 1892, containing the text of 82 tablets printed with the type of the Harrisons, with an introduction and summary of contents. (3) *Oriental Diplomacy*, Charles Bezold, London, 1893, contains a transliteration, and a résumé of the contents of the tablets in the British Museum, a valuable Introduction, setting forth many of the characteristic features of the language of these letters, and a Glossary. (4) *The Tell Amarna Tablets*, C. R. Conder, London, 1893, is of little scientific value. The articles in Hebraica, *ZA*, *PSBA*, *JBL*, etc., etc., need not be cited here.

The great mass of Assyrian Letters, however, belongs to the later period. The texts of a few are published in *The Cuneiform Inscriptions of Western Asia*, III. (1870), IV. (1875) and V. (1884).[1] Some Letters are transliterated and translated by George Smith in his *History of Assurbanipal* (1871).[2] His *Assyrian Discoveries* (1875) contains the translation of one letter.[3]

The next important work on the Letters is by Theo. G. Pinches (1) in *TSBA* VI. (1877), pp. 209–243, where he gives the text, transliteration, and translation of four Letters,[4] and (2) in *PSBA* (Nov. 1881) pp. 12–15, where he transliterates and translates two Letters.[5] The first article also contains some interesting and valuable general information on the Letter literature.

In *TSBA* VI. (June, 1877) pp. 289–304, a Letter[6] is published by H. F. Talbot in text, transliteration and translation with notes. The translation is reprinted in *RP* XI. (1878) pp. 99–104.

Pater Strassmaier has done a great service to Letter, as well as to other Assyrian, literature, in his *Alphabetisches Verzeichniss der Assyrischen und Akkadischen Wörter*, etc. (1886). This work contains much material from the Letters, chiefly from those Letters which were, at that time, unpublished. Some Letters are published in full, e. g. K. 280 on p. 813 sq. Many others are published in part.

Much more extensive work in this field than had yet been done was undertaken by S. A. Smith. In his *Keilschrifttexte Asurbanipals* II. (1887) and III. (1889) many Letters are found.[7] They are given in the text, with transliteration, translation and notes, and some supplementary notes by Pinches and Bezold.

This author has published other Letters, following the same plan of giving text, transliteration, translation and notes, in *PSBA* IX. (June 7, 1887) pp. 240–56; X. (Nov. 1, 1887) pp. 60–72; Jan. 10, 1888, pp. 155–77, and April, 1888, pp. 305–15.[8] These articles were reprinted and published under the title *Assyrian Letters*, Parts I.–IV. (1888).

---

[1] Vol. 3 contains K. 1619b and K. 1620b, (plate 16); vol. 4, K. 84, K. 13, and K. 647 (plate 52), K. 114, K. 31, and K. 79 (plate 53), K. 562, K. 528, K. 181, and 48-7-20, 15 (plate 54). In the new edition, 1891, these plates are nos. 45, 46, and 47. Vol. 5 has K. 186, K. 175, K. 618, K. 512 (plate 53). R^m. 2. 2, K. 613, K. 678, K. 537, K. 620 (plate 54).

[2] These are K. 1139 (p. 108 sq.), K. 312 (p. 189 sq.), part of K. 599 (p. 196 sq.), K. 13 (p. 197 sqq.), K. 10 (p. 248 sq.), K. 359 (p. 252 sqq.), K. 562 (p. 296 sqq.).

[3] Sm. 1034.

[4] These are K. 181, K. 528, K. 79 and K. 14.

[5] Viz. 80-7-19, 25 and 80-7-19, 26.

[6] K. 31.

[7] These are K. 538, K. 513, K. 562, K. 604, K. 476, 81-2-4, 57, K. 95, K. 486, K. 509, K. 312, K. 359, K. 524, S. 1064, K. 824, K. 11, K. 549, K. 183, K. 487, K. 525, K. 578, K. 646, K. 550, K. 1252[a], K. 533, K. 1249, S. 760, K. 96, K. 514, K. 679, K. 582, K. 686, K. 1220 and K. 1113, K. 660 and K. 1139.

[8] These are K. 482, K. 483, S. 1034, K. 82, K. 83, K. 691, K. 21, K. 80, K. 81, K. 89, K. 478, K. 481, K. 493, K. 498, K. 522, K. 113, K. 146, K. 174, K. 479, K. 492, K. 502, K. 504, K. 506, K. 507, K. 508, K. 511, K. 526, K. 154, K. 523, K. 572, K. 1122, 80-7-19, 17, R^m. 77. Besides these the text without translation is given of S. 1046 and 82-7-4, 37, the last being a contract tablet.

The work of Smith may be judged from different points of view. In many of the Letters, he has failed to grasp the central idea, and many of his explanations of particular words are unsatisfactory. A more thoroughly scientific grasp of the language would have led to better results. However, considering its value for the study of the Letter-literature, much may be said in its praise. The fact that the texts are very well transcribed is in itself a service of the first importance. Smith has made a great deal of material accessible to other investigators, and he has undoubtedly stimulated others, who, on the basis of his results, have been able to reach results differing, it is true, from his but more satisfactory.

In *ZA* II. (1887) pp. 58–68, two Letters[9] are published by C. F. Lehmann, under the title *Zwei Erlasse Asurbanabals.* These have text, transliteration, translation and notes.

Theo. G. Pinches, in his *Texts in the Babylonian Wedge-Writing*, Part I., has published the cuneiform text of several Letters.[10]

In the publication by C. Bezold of the *Catalogue of the Cuneiform Tablets of the Kouyunjik Collection of the British Museum*, I. (1889), II. (1891), III. (1894), a forward step is to be noted. These volumes greatly facilitate systematic study of the texts, which is indispensable in this branch of Assyriology. A preliminary service of a similar character had been rendered by his *Kurzgefasster Ueberblick über die Babylonisch-Assyrische Literatur.*

In the published portion of his *Assyrisches Wörterbuch* (1887–), Friedrich Delitzsch has given extracts from many Letters. His chief work upon them, however, is found in *Beiträge zur Assyriologie*, I., 1 (1889), pp. 185–248, I., 2 (1890), pp. 613–631 and II., 1, pp. 19–62.[11] These are published without the text, but with transliteration, translation and full notes. A large number of these texts had been previously treated by S. A. Smith, but the results here obtained mark a great advance beyond those of Smith. The work of Delitzsch is characterized by an acquaintance with the literature and by strict adherence to grammatical and lexicographical principles.

The scientific and systematic study of the Assyrian Letters was for the first time made possible to students in general through the publication of *The Assyrian and Babylonian Letters belonging to the K. Collection of the British Museum*, Part I. (1892), Part II. (1893), by Robert Francis Harper. The volumes so far published, which are part of a series, give the texts carefully transcribed, printed in type and arranged according to the names of the scribes. Volume I. contains 124

---

[9] K. 95 and 67-4-2, 1.

[10] These are K. 647, K. 10, K. 823, R^m. 215, K. 828, K. 831, K. 915, 80-7-19, 19.

[11] These articles contain K. 486, K. 523, K. 478, K. 476, K. 512, K. 81, K. 526, K. 146, 81-2-4, 57. K. 493, K. 498, K. 522, K. 572, K. 483, K. 604, K. 618, K. 95, 67-4-2, 1. K. 509, K. 82, Sm. 1034, K. 183, K. 601, K. 666, K. 583, K. 492, K. 482, K. 167, K. 11, K. 691, K. 507, K. 669, K. 479, K. 1113, K. 487, K. 549, K. 550, 80-7-19, 26, 80-7-19, 25, K. 525.

and volume II. 99 tablets, a total of 223 Letters.[12] Volume III. of this series will appear about October 1st, 1896.

Two Letters[13] have been treated by C. Johnston in *The Journal of the American Oriental Society*, XV., 3 (Apr. 22, 1892) pp. 311-16. They are transliterated and translated, and accompanied by a few notes. There is also a note on one of them, K. 84, by the same author in the *Johns Hopkins University Circulars* (June 1893) p. 108. Another Letter, S. 1064, is translated in *JHUC* (July 1894) p. 118 sq. Some general statements about the epistolary literature are given by him in *JHUC* (July 1894) p. 119 sq.

Several Letters are published in the cuneiform text by Hugo Winckler in *Sammlung von Keilschrifttexten*, II., 1 (1893) and II., 2 (1894).[14] These contain many mistakes in copying. The editor's excuse in the preface of the last part to the effect that he had compared his copies with the original text but once, is an aggravation of the offense, for it is well nigh unpardonable for a man to publish such texts without taking every precaution to insure their correctness.

A few other miscellaneous references may be grouped together here. J. Menant, in his *Manuel de la Langue Assyrienne* (1880), has published K. 562. Part of K. 154 is published with transliteration, translation and notes, by H. F. Talbot in *TSBA* I., 16 sqq., 352 sq. Extracts from K. 177 are published by Lenormant in *Essai sur un document mathematique*, p. 74. A translation of K. 562 is given by Delitzsch in *Wo lag das Paradies?* 302 sq. Part of K. 605 is published with transliteration and translation by Pinches in *PSBA*, V., 28. A transliteration

---

[12] These are K. 11, K. 14, K. 21, K. 63b, K. 80, K. 83, K. 89, K. 112, K. 113, K. 117, K. 122, K. 125, K. 146, K. 167, K. 174, K. 175, K. 181, K. 183, K. 185, K. 186, K. 194, K. 466, K. 467, K. 468, K. 469, K. 472, K. 476, K. 481, K. 482, K. 483, K. 485, K. 487, K. 488, K. 490, K. 491, K. 492, K. 494, K. 495, K. 497, K. 499, K. 501, K. 503, K. 504, K. 505, K. 507, K. 511, K. 512, K. 515, K. 518, K. 519, K. 520, K. 522, K. 527, K. 529, K. 530, K. 532, K. 537, K. 538, K. 539, K. 540, K. 541, K. 542, K. 546, K. 547, K. 549, K. 550, K. 551, K. 553, K. 554, K. 555, K. 558, K. 561, K. 565, K. 568, K. 569, K. 572, K. 573, K. 574, K. 575, K. 576, K. 577, K. 582, K. 583, K. 584, K. 589, K. 591, K. 594, K. 595, K. 596, K. 598, K. 601, K. 602, K. 604, K. 606, K. 609, K. 612, K. 613, K. 614, K. 616, K. 617, K. 618, K. 619, K. 620, K. 623, K. 624, K. 625, K. 626, K. 627, K. 629, K. 631, K. 636, K. 639, K. 641, K. 642, K. 643, K. 647, K. 649, K. 650, K. 652, K. 653, K. 655, K. 656, K. 657, K. 660, K. 662, K. 664, K. 665, K. 666, K. 679, K. 682, K. 686, K. 687, K. 690, K. 691, K. 831, K. 903, K. 910, K. 939a, K. 970, K. 979, K. 981, K. 983, K. 991, K. 997, K. 1000, K. 1013, K. 1017, K. 1019, K. 1022, K. 1024, K. 1025, K. 1028, K. 1032, K. 1033, K. 1037, K. 1039, K. 1040, K. 1041, K. 1047, K. 1048, K. 1049, K. 1050, K. 1052, K. 1053, K. 1057, K. 1058, K. 1060, K. 1062, K. 1067, K. 1069, K. 1070, K. 1080, K. 1082, K. 1087, K. 1101 and K. 1221, K. 1113 and K. 1229, K. 1147 and K. 1947, K. 1151, K. 1168, K. 1170, K. 1187, K. 1189, K. 1195, K. 1197, K. 1199, K. 1200, K. 1204, K. 1205, K. 1209, K. 1234, K. 1235, K. 1239, K. 1242, K. 1243, K. 1267, K. 1270, K. 1272, K. 1274, K. 1396, K. 1410, K. 1418, K. 1428, K. 1461, K. 1540, K. 1896, K. 1907, K. 2,909, K. 4281, K. 4304, K. 4703, K. 4704, K. 4770, K. 4780, K. 5244b, K. 5458, K. 5464, K. 5465, K. 5466, K. 5509, K. 5531, K. 7426, K. 7434, K. 7493.

[13] K. 828 and K. 84.

[14] These are K. 1106, K. 1355, K. 5464, K. 2701a, K. 233, K. 1067, K. 1080, K. 176, K. 5425[a], K. 112, K. 1037, K. 2889, K. 125, K. 1107, K. 1621b, K. 1118, K. 1374, K. 1459, K. 1541, K. 1542, K. 1904, K. 1610, K. 17, K. 168, K. 1550, K. 1580, K. 1287, K. 97, K. 1199, K. 4287, K. 4303, K. 1174, K. 1247, K. 94, K. 1196, K. 1066, K. 1238, K. 1210, K. 4682, K. 4724, K. 1197 [1187], K. 1062, K. 1202, K. 1201, K. 1146, K. 1247, K. 1366, K. 63b, K. 844, K. 1239, K. 4757, K. 1274, K. 4785, K. 5461, K. 5333b, K. 87, K. 1164, K. 5457, K. 2645, K. 4779, K. 4670, K. 1263, K. 1250, K. 830, 1895, K. 1176, K. 1271, K. 1265, K. 894, K. 1335, K. 1077, K. 896, K. 1269, K. 1065, K. 4776, K. 5473, K. 4775, K. 5483, K. 1880, K. 1881, K. 4787, K. 4793, K. 5594, K. 5585, K. 5550 and K. 5641, K. 5500.

and translation of K. 1619b is given by Sayce in *Babylonian Literature*, p. 78, and by Amiaud in *Babylonian and Oriental Record*, II., 197 sqq. The text of K. 1620b with transliteration and translation has been published by Budge, *History of Esarhaddon*, 14 sq.

The cuneiform text of the Letters here considered was published by Robert Francis Harper in *ZA*, VIII. (1893) pp. 341–59.

The best information obtainable places the number of Letter tablets in the British Museum at over one thousand, of which less than half have been published. Their difficulty has often been emphasized. Undoubtedly the short notes containing accounts of the transportation of horses and other animals present the least difficulty. Military reports are deciphered with considerable ease, while the Letters upon astrological subjects are most difficult. In fact, they are often quite unintelligible. A few are dated, but only with the month and day, so that they give no help in determining the date of composition. How the date, in such cases, may be determined, however, Bezold has shown in *Die Thontafelsammlungen des British Museum* (1888), p. 14 sqq. The method suggested by him will be increasingly successful as the decipherment progresses.

There is no section of Assyrian literature which requires more patient, systematic and well directed labor for the solution of its problems. But it is not too much to expect that ultimately these Letter tablets, on account of their number, the variety of their contents, and the light which they throw upon the everyday side of life, will contribute much material of great value for the real history of Assyria and Babylonia.

Most of those who have written upon the Letters have attempted to give a complete translation in each case. It must be confessed, however, that these attempts have not been particularly successful. The difficulty of many of the Letters is such that to attempt a connected translation in our present state of knowledge is almost a waste of time. I have, therefore, in the following pages deemed it best, not to give translations, but rather a complete glossary, following in this the example of Bezold in his *Oriental Diplomacy*.

To my teacher, Professor Robert Francis Harper, I am greatly indebted for valuable suggestions and help in my study of these texts. For the conclusions reached, however, I alone am responsible.

TRANSLITERATION.

R^{M} 2, 1.

OBVERSE.

1 A-na šarri bêli-ia 2 ardu-ka $^{m\ ilu}$ Šamaš-bêl-uṣur 3 lu šul-mu a-na šarri bêli-ia 4 ina muḫḫi ka-li-ia ša šarru be-ili 5 ištu $^{m\ alu}$ Arba-ilu-a-a iš-pur-an-ni 6 ma a-ta-a ka-li-ia-u la-šu 7 ki-i ištu ^{m} Išdi-ḫarrâni ^{amêlu} mutîr

pu-te 8 i-li-kan-a-ni a-na ^{alu} Ur-zu-ḫi-na 9 i-[na] pa-na-tu-šu-nu II ^{imêru} ku-din
10 ina šapli ^m Išid-ḫarrâni ar-ta-kas 11 ina ^{alu} Arrapḫa i-ṣa-bat II ^{imêru} ku-
din 12 ina šapli ^m Arba-ilu-a-a ir-ta-kas 13 a-na ^{mâtu} Ma-ṣa-mu i-ta-lak
14 šarru be-ili ar........ma-la 15 u-ru-u ša [imêru ina] ^{alu} Dûr-ta-li-ti 16
u-ru-u ša ^{imêru} ku-din ina ^{alu} Ta-ga-la-gi 17 u-ša-zi-zu-u-ni 18 ištu ^{alu} Ur-zu-
ḫi-na i-tu-ṣi 19 II ^{imêru} ku-din ina šapli-šu ka-li-ia-u 20 a-na ka-li-e a-di
^{alu} A-ra-ak-di 21 ki-i u-ma-a i-li-kan-a-ni 22 bid šarru be-ili iš-pur-šu-u-ni
23 a-na-ku ina ^{alu} Ur-zu-ḫi-na 24 II ^{imêru} ku-din ina šap[li] 25 ar-ta-kas.

REVERSE.

1 a-di ^{alu} Dûr-ta-[li-ti] 2 .... 3 ....
4 šarru be-ili u-da 5 ki-i ^{alu} Ar-zu-ḫi-na 6 ina libbi ^{işu} pi-lu-ur-te 7 ka-
ri-ru-u-ni mar-di-tu 8 ištu ^{alu} Ur-zu-ḫi-na-a-di 9 ^{alu} A-ra-ak-di a-na u-ma-
me 10 ta-da-in šarru be-ili- 11 a ṭe-mu ši-kun 12 ka-li-ia-u 13 ina ^{alu} Dûr-t
atânâ ^{pl.}-te 14 lu-ša-zi-zu a-ḫi-ia-ši 15 uu-ti-in ina muḫḫi ^{amêlu} zammêrê ^{pl.}
16 ša šarru be-ili iš-pur-an-ni 17 ma-a ina muḫḫi ^{amêlu} mârâ ^{pl.}-ni 18 ša ^{amêlu}
rab-SE-ŠA ina ^{mâtu} Ba-bi-ti 19 i-tu-uḳ-tu a-sa-al 20 u-ta-ṣi-ṣi me-me-[ni]
la-šu 21 u la ni-iš-me šarru be-ili 22 i-šap-ra ma-a šum-ma ^{amêlu} zammêrê ^{pl.}
23 ba tu-ṣa-bit ma-a lu tu-da 24 ki-i ap-ta tu-šal-lum-ni 25 ^{amêlu} pa-ri-ṣu-u-te
26 ša ^{alu} Arrapḫa 27 ša bît ^{amêlu} nâgir ekalli 28 up-ta-at-ḫu-ru ina libbi
šum-ṣa ḳu-bu u-ma ..... 29 u-si-li i-na-ṣur šum-ma u-ṣa-bit-u-ni 30
u-bal-u-ni-šu-nu a-nu-ši m ^{amêlu} zammêrê ^{pl.} ša bît ^{amêlu}........ 31 ša ḳa-an-
ni ^{alu} Ur-zu-ḫi-na šarru be-ili ina pân šarri bêli-[ia]........

R^M 2, 2.

OBVERSE.

1 Duppu ^m Gil-ṣa-na 2 a-na ^{amêlu} nâgir bîti 3 lu šul-mu a-na-ka 4 ša
taš-pur-an-ni 5 ma-a šar ^{mâtu} Akkad-a-a 6 a-di ^{amêlu} e-muḳ-ḳi-šu 7 kar-
ka-te-e i-lak 8 ma-a a-a-ka u-šab 9 ^{amêlu} bêl piḫâti ša ^{alu} U-a-si 10 ^{amêlu}
bêl piḫâti ša ḳa-ni ^{mâtu} U-ka-a-a 11 i-tal-ku-u-ni dul-lu 12 ina aširti e-pu-šu
13 i-da-bu-ub ma-a šarru 14 i-lak ina ^{alu} U-a-si u-šab 15 ma-a ^{amêlu} bêl
piḫâtê ^{pl.} uḫ-ḫu-ru 16 i-la-ku-u-ni

REVERSE.

1 ina ^{alu} Mu-ṣa-ṣir 2 dul-lu e-pu-šu 3 ša taš-pur-an-ni 4 ma-a ša la pi-i
5 ša šarri me-me-ni 6 it-[ti]-šu ina dul-li 7 lu la u-ba-la 8 ki-i šar ^{mâtu}
Aššur (ki) 9 i-lik-an-ni ak-tal-šu-u 10 ša e-pu-šu-ni e-tap-ša 11 u an-ni-u
a-ki-e 12 kil-la-šu.

R^M 2, 3.

OBVERSE.

1 A-na šarri b[e-ili-ia] 2 ardu-ka ^m Ašur-ri-ṣu-a 3 lu šul-mu a-na šarri
be-ili-ia 4 3000 ^{amêlu} ṣâbê ^{pl.} šêpâ ^{pl.} 5 amêlu ša-nu-te ^{amêlu} rab-šabrê ^{pl.} 6

ša m Si-e-ti-ni amêlu bêl piḫâti 7 ša pu-tu ellu a-na alu Mu-ṣa-ṣir 8 u-ta-me-šu nâru ME 9 e-tab-ru imêru a-ṣap-pu-šu 10 .... še ma-la ša m Si-e-ti-ni 11 ina pa-ni-šu šu-u 12 ša m Su-na-a 13 amêlu bêl piḫâti.

REVERSE.

1 ša pu-ut mâtu U-ka-a-a 2 amêlu ṣâbê pl.-šu 3 u-ta-mi-šu-ma 4 a-na alu Mu-ṣa-ṣir 5 a-si-me ma-a šarru 6 ina libbi alu U-e-si 7 il-lak u-di-na 8 la u-nam-maš.

RM 2, 4.

OBVERSE.

1 A-na šarri bêli-ia 2 ardu-ka m Šam-ḫu ilu Ša-maš 3 lu-u šul-mu 4 a-na šarri bêli-ia 5 ina muḫḫi amêlu šakan-maṣṣarti 6 ša ištu amêlu da-gil-iṣṣurê pl. 7 ša šarru be-ili 8 iš-pur-an-ni 9 ma-a ina pâni-ka 10 lu-uk-ta-ti-ni 11 ma-a mi-i-nu 12 ša ištu pân amêlu da-gil-iṣṣurê pl. 13 i-šu-u-ni 14 lu-u-sa-ḫi-ri 15 [l]id-din

REVERSE.

1 a-sa-'a-la 2 u-ta-ṣi 3 me-me-ni ...... 4 ištu pa-ni-šu-nu 5 la i....ši-i 6 ina muḫḫi.....pu-na 7 u-ma-a a-ki ša šarru 8 bêli iḳ-bu-u-ni 9 amêlu šakan-maṣṣarti ur-ki-ia-u 10 ina pâni-šu-nu 11 ak-ta-la 12 am-me-ia-u 13 a-na maṣṣarti-šu 14 i-ta-ta-ka

RM 2, 5.

OBVERSE.

1 A-na šarri bêli-a 2 ardu-ka m A-bit-šar-uṣur 3 lu šul-mu a-na šarri bêli-a 4 ina muḫḫi m ilu Nabû-er-eš 5 amêlu Kal-da-a-a 6 ša šarru be-ili iš-pur-an-ni 7 ma-a šap-li ḳa-ti 8 ma-ṣar-tu-šu uṣ-ṣu-ru 9 ištu mar šarru be-ili 10 iš-pur-an-ni 11 a-sa-par ma-ṣar-tu-šu 12 šap-la ḳa-ti 13 it-ta-aṣ-ru.

REVERSE.

1 u-ma-a 2 an-nu-ri 3 u-tam-me-ša 4 il-la-ka 5 ma-a a-na šul-me 6 ina ekalli al-lak

RM 2, 6.

OBVERSE.

1 A-na šarri bêli-ia 2 ardu-ka m Ištar-šum-er-eš 3 lu šul-mu a-na šarri bêli-ia 4 ilu Nabû u ilu Marduk 5 a-na šarri bêli-ia lik-ru-bu 6 ša šarru be-li iš-pur-an-ni 7 ma-a u-la ina bi-rit pu-ri-di 8 a-me-li e-ti-iḳ 9 ina muḫḫi ša šap-la išu narkabti-e 10 tu-ṣu-u-ni ina muḫ-ḫi-šu 11 šarru be-li i-ḳab-[bi] .... 12 ma-a pu-ri-di .... 13 pu-ri-di ki-ma .... 14 ša amêlu u .... 15 šu-u bi-r[it] .... 16 is-[su]-ri ma(?)........ 17 u........ 18 ....

REVERSE.

1 a-na it-ti........... 2 nu-ka-al šu-u an......... 3 ištu KAT a-na kan........ 4 šap-la ^{iṣu} narkabti it........ 5 ša pu-ri-di...... 6 ša šarru be-li [iḳ-bu-u-ni] .... 7 an-ni-u pi........ 8 ^{m ilu} Beltu-kab-din ina bi .... 9 ḳitridu ^{amêlu} e........ 10 lu-u kiššat ili lu-u kiššat šarri mat-su 11 a-ḫu-lam-ma ^{amêlu} Aš-da(?)-a-a-ti 12 ni-iḳ-bi a-ta-a 13 la šarrâni ^{pl.} nak-ru-ti-šu-nu 14 šap-la ^{iṣu} mu-gir-ri 15 ša šarri bêli-ia 16 la i-ka-an-nu-šu

R^M 2, 7.

1 A-na šarri [bêli-ia] 2 ardu-ka ^{m} Šar .... 3 lu šul-mu a-na šarri be-[ili-ia] 4 ^{m} Bab-ba-ni ^{amêlu} [mutîr pu-te] 5 70 ṣâbê ^{pl.} tabê ^{pl.} .... 6 ^{mâtu} Akkadi (ki) a........ 7 na-ṣa ina ^{alu} .... 8 uš-še-si .... 9 u ṣâbê ^{pl.}........ 10 id-da-àb ^{mâtu} 11 ma-a u........ 12 ištu pa-ni .... 13 iḫ-ri........

R^M 2, 8.

OBVERSE.

1 A-na šarri be-ili-ia 2 ardu-ka ^{m ilu} Nabû-šum-iddina 3 lu šul-mu a-na šarri be-ili-ia 4 a-dan-niš a-dan-niš 5 ^{ilu} Nabû ^{ilu} Marduk 6 a-na šarri be-ili-ia lik-ru-bu 7 ^{ilu} Bêl ^{ilu} Nabû ^{ilu} Nergal 8 nu-[um-mur] ša šarri 9 be-ili-[ia] li-iṣ-ṣu-ru 10 [šar-ru]-u-tu ša šarri 11 [be-ili-ia ana 100] šanâti ^{pl.} 12 [a-na šarri be-ili-ia] lu-ki-in-nu 13 .... ki-e-ni at-ta 14 ....nu šar-ru-u-tu 15 a-na li-pi-i-ka 16 a-na zi-ri-ka 17 a-na ṣa-at ûme 18 [lid-di]-nu 19 .... bit-ḫal-li

REVERSE.

1 .... ṣap-pa 2 .... bit-ḫal-li 3 [ištu ^{alu} D]ûr-Šar-ukîn 4 .... ûmu an-ni-u 5 e-tar-bu-u-ni 6 mu-šu an-ni[-u e]-pu-šu 7 ša ti-[ma]-a-li 8 sisê ^{pl.} as-si-kal 9 a-na mi-i-ni ka-a-a-ma-ni-u 10 sisê ^{pl.} ša šarri u-ša-ad-la-ab 11 šum-ma šarru be-ili i-ḳab-bi 12 sisê ^{pl.} la-as-kal 13 mi-i-nu ša šarru be-ili 14 i-šap-par-an-ni 15 ûmi 23

R^M 2, 11.

OBVERSE.

[Several lines broken away.]

1 ša šarru be-ili......... 2 ma-a šu-pur li... ...... 3 lu-u-bi-lu-ni-šu a-sa-[al] 4 ina ^{mâtu} Bar-ḫal-ṣa up-ta-ṣi.... 5 la-a-šu la-a e-mu-ru-šu 6 a-na ^{alu} Mu-ti-an-ni 7 ina libbi ali-šu it-tal-ka 8 la-a-aš-šu 9 aḫu-šu šu-u-tu 10 e-du-ma-nu ina lib-bi

REVERSE.

1 kam-mu-su i-ṣab-tu 2 na-ṣu-ni-šu a-sa-al-šu 3 nu-uk aḫu-ka a-li-e 4 ma-a la il-li-kam-ma ina muḫ-ḫi-a 5 an-nu-šim........ šarri bêli-a 6 u-si-bi .... 7 u amêlu ma........ 8 ina muḫḫi m Di........

[Several lines broken away.]

RM 2, 458.

OBVERSE.

1 A-na šarri bêli-ia 2 ardu-ka m Tâbu-ṣil-Ešarra 3 šul-mu a-na Ešarra (ki) 4 šul-mu a-na ekurrâte 5 šul-mu a-na alu Aššur 6 šul-mu a-na mâtu Aš-šur (ki) 7 lu šul-mu a-na šarri bêli-ia 8 Ašur ilu Bêltu a-na šarri bêli-ia 9 lik-ru-bu ina muḫḫi iṣu gušûrê pl. 10 ša šarru iš-pur-an-ni

[Several lines broken away.]

REVERSE.

[Several lines broken away.]

1 .... 2 ...... a-dan-niš 3 ...... u-ma-ni-e 4 ma-a-du iṣu gušûrê pl. 5 lib-bu ša šarri .... bêli-ia 6 lu-u tâb

RM 2, 459.

1 [A-na] šarri bêli-i[a] 2 [ardu]-ka m Tâbu-ṣil-E[šarra] 3 [l]u šul-mu a-na šarri bêli-[ia] 4 Ašur ilu Bêltu a-na šarri b[êli-ia] 5 lik-ru-bu ina muḫḫi iṣu [gušûrê pl.] 6 ša šarru be-ili iš-pur-a[n-ni] 7 ma-a šu-pur liš-da-du .... 8 a-du la-a šarru be-ili .... 9 .... u-ta-si ....

[Several lines broken away.]

RM 2, 462.

1 [A-na šarri bêli-a] 2 ardu-ka m Ašur-dûr-pa-ni-[a] 3 lu-u šul-mu a-na šarri bêli-a 4 ištu muḫḫi m Abû-ul-i-di 5 amêlu mutîr pu-te mâtu Kal-da-a-a 6 ša šarru bêli iš-pur-an-ni 7 ma-[a] .... su........

[Several lines broken away.]

RM 2, 463.

1 A-na šarri be-ili-ia 2 ardu-ka m Šamaš-emur-an-ni 3 lu-u šul-mu a-na šarri bêli-ia 4 šul-mu a-na alu Ḫal-ṣu 5 ša šarru be-ili iš-pur-an-ni 6 ma-a 50 amêlu Kur-ra-a-a 7 50 amêlu I-tu-'-a-a 8 ina alu Sa-ba-ḫa-ni 9 šup-ru a-šap-ra 10 amêlu ṣâbê pl. ša amêlu rab-bi-lul 11 ša ina libbi .... 12 la i........ 13 la-u .... 14 [m]i-nu .... 15 be-ili .... 16 liš pa-r[u]

R^{M} 2, 464.

OBVERSE.

[Several lines broken away.]

1 .... 2 ina ûmi 18 $^{\text{[kan]}}$ ša....... 3 ^{alu} Kâr-^{m} Šar-ukîn.... 4 a-na maṣṣarâti$^{\text{pl.}}$ gab........... 5 šul-mu ^{amêlu} ḫazân[âte] 6 ša bat-ti-bat-ti-e-a šul-mu........ 7 i-sa-al-lu ina muḫḫi ṭe-e-[mu] 8 ša ^{m} Lu-tu-u šu-u-tu 9 ^{m} Aš-pa-ba-ra ina ^{alu} Ḫa-ri-pa 10 ḳa-ra-bu i-sa-ḫa ia-ši 11 u-pu-šu ^{amêlu} ṣâbê$^{\text{pl.}}$ ša a-ḫa-ia-ši 12 i-du-u-ku ina muḫḫi ^{m} Up-pi-te 13 ^{amêlu} ḫazânu ša ^{alu} Ur-ia-ku 14 ša pa-tu-u-ni 15 ša a-na šarri bêli-a 16 a-ḳa-bu-u-ni

REVERSE.

1 ki-i a-na-ku ina pa-ni-t[u-šu] 2 al-lik-an-ni šu-u-tu 3 a-na ^{mâtu} Ša-maš-da iḫ-tal-ḳa 4 ^{m} ^{ilu} Nabu-lal-an-ni ^{amêlu} NA 5 ša šarru i-si-mi šu-u-tu 6 ^{m} U-ak-sa-tar i-sa-ap-ru 7 iṣ-ṣab-tu-ni-šu 4 ^{amêlu} mârâni$^{\text{pl.}}$-šu 8 is-si-e-šu ina libbi ûmu 9 ša a-na-ku a-na ^{alu} Kâr-^{m} Šar-ukîn 10 e-ru-bu-u-ni ina muḫḫi ^{m} Ra-ma....i 11 a-sa-ap-ra šum-ku-un .... 12 še-bi-la ki-ma iṣ-ṣa........ 13 na-ṣu-u-ni a-na........

[Several lines broken away.]

NOTES.

R^{M} 2, 1.

OBVERSE l. 4.—The sign muḫ may be read either eli or muḫḫi. It is usually read eli except where a phonetic complement makes this impossible. I think in the letters that it should everywhere be read muḫḫi. The reason is, that it is frequently found written muḫ-ḫi, both by itself and before pronominal suffixes.[1] It may be a question whether we have here syllabic writing, or an ideogram and phonetic complement. So far as I know, it is never written with any other phonetic complement which would indicate the reading eli; nor is eli found written syllabically in the letters. ka-li-ia occurs in this letter in two other forms, ka-li-e, l. 20, and the fullest form, ka-li-ia-u, ls. 6, 19, rev. 12. *u* at the end can not be a separate word, cf. l. 19. A word kalû=*priest*, is given by Zimmern, *BB.* (p. 28, note 2), which is not suitable here. Delitzsch, *Heb. Lang.* p. 25, gives the word kalû, *vessel*, synonym of unûtu, Hebrew כְּלִי, without

[1] For muḫ-ḫi, by itself, cf. K. 502:11, K. 981: rev. 6, *LK.* 34; K. 492:5, *LK.* 3; Sm. 1034:7, *BAS.*, I., 2, p. 614; K. 1025:4, *LK.* 159; K. 505:6, *LK.* 166; K. 575: rev. 10, *LK.* 177; K. 1058: 4, *LK.* 182; K. 1000:5, *LK.* 188; K. 222: rev. 21, *LK.* 222; K. 1024: rev. 7, *LK.* 28; K. 1204, rev. 4, *LK.* 29; K. 174: rev. 9, *LK.* 53; K. 687:13, *LK.* 57. For muḫ-ḫi-ia, cf. K. 507:12, *LK.* 88; K. 526:10, K. 498:6, K. 503:5, *LK.* 125; K. 686:6, 8, *LK.* 173; K. 662: 15, *LK.* 211 (a peculiar form): R^{m}. 2, 11: rev. 4 (muḫ-ḫi-a); K. 5466: rev. 8, *LK.* 90. For muḫ-ḫi-šu, R^{m}. 2, 6:10, K. 530:10, 15, *LK.* 158. For muḫ-ḫi-šu-nu, cf. K. 582:20, *LK.* 167; K. 679: rev. 10, *LK.* 212.

examples. In his *Handwörterbuch* he omits k a l û, giving only k a l û t u in this sense. I accept Delitzsch's derivation here, giving a broad meaning, as in Hebrew. The general meaning, *preparation for war*, or for *march*, is very appropriate here. For a similar meaning in Hebrew, cf. Jer. 46:19. One may take i a - u as equivalent to i u,[2] which might have been still further contracted to k a l û. The other forms of the word then give no difficulty; k a - l i - i a is the accusative, k a - l i - e the genitive.

l. 5. It is interesting to note the separation between the wedges of the first character. It is undoubtedly to be read i š t u.

l. 6. The character *a* is intended to do double duty. The scribe meant to say m a - a a - t a - a. Such things are common in the letters.[3] l a - š u. The form is l â š û. This is the usual form in the letters, contracted from l â i š î, or l â i š û of the historical inscriptions. l â i š î uncontracted occurs rarely in the letters.[4] On the other hand, l â š û sometimes occurs in the historical inscriptions.[5] The writing in the letters varies much.[6]

l. 7. m u t î r p u - t e—The meaning and various writings of this word have been discussed by Delitzsch.[7]

l. 8. i - l i - k a n - a - n i. A peculiar writing=i l i k a n i; cf. also l. 21 below. Like t a b - r a t - a - t i, cf. *DG.*, § 23 note. U r z u ḫ i n a.—Delitzsch[8] correctly identifies this form with the more common A r z u ḫ i n a. It is interesting to note it in this letter as the usual form, occurring here and in ls. 18, 23, and rev. 8, 31, while A r z u ḫ i n a occurs once, in rev. 5.

l. 9. It seems evident that n a is simply omitted by the scribe. There is no break in the text. Such omissions are not uncommon in the letters.

l. 9. imêru k u - d i n. For the reading and meaning of this word, cf. Zehnpfund, *BAS.*, I, 2, p. 505, note, where references to other passages are given.

l. 11. i - ṣ a - b a t must be taken as a Pres. This fact shows that the parallel i - t a - l a k, l. 13, is probably to be considered a Pres., although the Pret. has the same form.

l. 14. The most probable conjecture for the break would be u - d a, which is often found in places like this, cf. rev. 4. But that does not suit the portion which is legible.

l. 15. The break does not seem sufficiently large for any more than I have supplied. D û r - T a - l i - t i = *wall of nativity*, an interesting name for a city.

---

[2] For a similar form cf. l u - š a r - b i - i a - u, K. 575: 7, *LK.* 177, the usual form of which is l u - š a r - b i - u, K. 510: 12, *LK.* 113; K. 538: 13, *LK.* 114, etc.

[3] Cf. K. 490: 7, *LK.* 18, m a - a - n a = m a - a a - n a.

[4] Cf. Rm. 2, 4: rev. 5.

[5] Cf. l a - a š - š u, TP. 7: 25.

[6] The most frequent writing is l a - a š - š u; K. 183: rev. 17, *LK.* 2; K. 186: rev. 17, *LK.* 222; K. 522: 13, *LK.* 31; K. 657: 9, *LK.* 102; K. 903: rev. 4, *LK.* 124; K. 491: 9, *LK.* 122, etc. Also l a - a - a š - š u, Rm. 2, 11: 8; l a - a - š u, Rm. 2, 11: 5; for l a - š u, cf. also rev. 20 below.

[7] Cf. *BAS.*, I. 1. p. 203.

[8] *BAS.*, I. 1. pp. 206-7.

l. 19. ka-li-ia-u a-na ka-li-e means evidently, *provision in abundance*.[9]

l. 22. bid. Occurs frequently in the letters and is practically equivalent to kî, *as, when*, cf. *BAS.*, I., 1. p. 205-6.

REVERSE l. 7.—karirûni, Perm. from כרר. This root occurs several times, chiefly in the letters.[10] S. A. Smith, *PSBA.*, 1886–7, p. 246, gives the meaning *repair*. Delitzsch *BAS.*, I., 2, p. 616, gives *einreissen, niederreissen*. Neither suits all the passages. Here the word seems to have a passive meaning, *is situated*. Its subject apparently is Arzuḫina.

l. 7. mar-di-tu. A good מ-formation with fem. ending from רדה, *to tread, march*, exactly like maršîtu, *possession*, etc. It would then seem that it should mean either *march*, or *way, road*. I prefer the latter.

l. 9. u-ma-me, *wild beasts*, furnishes a key to the thought here.

l. 10. ta-da-in. If this were tudain, it would suggest a II. 1. form from a root דון, or דין, cf. the common form uka'in, but this form would naturally be I. 1. The root is perhaps נדן, nadânu, *to give*. The form da-in is then for din, a form comparatively common in the letters. It can hardly be called an irregularity; it is more correct to say that the letters do not demand that a vowel be always followed by the same vowel. For a noun, tadanu=*gift*, cf. *BAS.*, I., 1, p. 282. Note the very unusual division of a word at the end of a line.

l. 11. ši-kun. I am disposed to regard this as a Perm. from šakânu. It is a bad form, but it is not without analogy.[11]

l. 17. We see here an extension of the use of determinatives beyond that found in the historical inscriptions, but precisely similar to that found in the Tel el-Amarna tablets. Other examples may be given.[12]

l. 18. cf. Ašurnaṣirpal, 2:33, 34.

l. 20. u-ta-ṣi-ṣi from יצא II., 2 might possibly be taken as a quadriliteral formed by reduplication of the last radical, cf. *DG.*, § 117, 2) a). It is better, however, to regard it as a simple repetition of the last sign by the scribe.

---

[9] For a similar expression, cf. šêpu ana šêpi, K. 14, rev. 13, *LK.* 42.

[10] The passages known to me are these, ka-ri-ru-u-ni, K. 5466: rev. 8, *LK.* 99; karru Ep. Y, 788; ka-ra-ri, K. 494:5, *LK.* 19; Sm. 1034:12; li-ik-ru-ur, Sm. 1034:18; li-ik-ru-ra, K. 494:12, *LK.* 19; ik-ta-ru-ar, K. 122: rev. 13, *LK.* 43; ak-ta-ra-ra, K. 655: rev. 5, *LK.* 132.

[11] Cf. The Permansive forms given in Bezold, *Oriental Diplomacy* p. XXIX, thus, ṣabat, ṣiḫir, šulmat, and similar forms. Cf. also *ZA.*, V. pp. 13-21. This form is parallel to ṣiḫir as qatul to qatil, cf. *DG.*, § 89 and also *ZA.*, V. p. 9, note 3. Another unusual form of permansive in the letters which may be cited is ḳa-ra-bu, R^m. 2, 464: 10, like ṣabat. Cf. also, outside of the letters, ni-bu-u, TP. 1:35, ḳi-bir, etc.

[12] Cf. (amêlu) mâru, K. 617:15, *LK.* 208 (in contrast with l. 11, where amêlu is not found). Also amêlu ardu, K. 122:6, *LK.* 43; K. 939a: 6, *LK.* 46; K. 604:13, *LK.* 44; K. 618:14, *LK.* 9; (amêlu) ardâni, K. 596:7, 18, 20, 22, 26, rev. 3, 12, 19, *LK.* 190: K. 617: rev. 14, *LK.* 208: K. 679: rev. 6, *LK.* 212; K. 1062: rev. 7, *LK.* 216; K. 507: rev. 21, *LK.* 88. Cf. also the plural sign with amêlu *pl.*, amêlu šâmûti K. 5466: rev. 12, *LK.* 99. All these uses have their parallels in the Tel el-Amarna tablets, cf. Bezold, *Oriental Diplomacy*, p. XVI.

l. 20. me-me.—ni is evidently omitted by the scribe.

l. 20. The reading given for this line is confirmed by passages closely parallel.[13]

l. 23. ba is probably a mistake of the scribe, and is to be considered as erased.

l. 25. pa-ri-ṣu-u-te. From פרץ =probably *judges*.[14]

l. 27. nâgir, undoubtedly so to be read, although it is actually the sign for nîru, *yoke*.

l. 28. up-ta-at-ḫu-ru, II. 2 Pret. of. paḫâru, with doubled t, cf. *DG*., §83, note. ḫuru is for the usual ḫiru.[15]

l. 28. ḳu-bu, cf. K. 485, rev. 13, *LK*. 112. Probably this is ḳubbû (קבא) *cry*.

l. 30. a-nu-šim. The word is a very common one in the letters. Usually written an-nu-šim, yet several times a-nu-šim.

l. 31. ḳa-an-ni. Taken up both by S. A. Smith, and Delitzsch in *BAS*., II., 1. p. 60. Smith derives it from קנה, *nest*. Delitzsch takes it from the root קוה, making it pl. of ḳu, but gives no translation. Neither can be considered entirely correct. The writing in this passage renders it improbable that it is from קוה. I offer no derivation, but I think the meaning is reasonably certain. It has a meaning and usage very similar to put, i. e. *entrance*, *side*. The way in which it is used with names of countries, and, in this passage, of a city, shows this, cf. R^m. 2, 2:10, with R^m. 2, 3: rev. 1.

---

[13] Cf. R^m. 2, 4: rev. 1-5, and R^m. 2, 11: 3-5, especially 5.

[14] Distinguish this word from (amêlu) par-ri-ṣu, in K. 617: 17, *LK*. 208.

[15] Many roots are found which have a different ultimate vowel in the letters from that which had been known elsewhere. This occurs chiefly in the I., 1. Preterite. Some cases occur in the historical inscriptions, and have usually been classed as irregularities. Some of these occur so frequently in the same form in the letters that they can not be considered simply mistakes, but show a current, although it may be colloquial, form. Together with this, it is true, there is much variation in vowels in the letters which may be ascribed simply to carelessness and inaccuracy. Some examples of verbal forms found with an ultimate vowel in the letters different from the usual one elsewhere are the following: iš-ka-nu-u-ni, K. 14: rev. 3, *LK*. 42, I., 1. pret. for iškununi; i-ša-ku-nu, K. 14: rev. 14, *LK*. 42, I., 1. Pret. or Pres., either for iškunu, or išákanu; cf. also, for the Pret. iš-ka-nu-ni, Ašurn., 2:83 (where Winckler writes "sic!"), and ni-iš-kan, Bezold, *Orient. Dipl.*, p. 112; e-pa-ši, K. 691: rev. 5, *LK*. 45. I., 1, Inf. and e-pa-aš-u-ni, K. 691: rev. 8, *LK*. 45, I., 1. Pret. or Pres. instead of the usual epêši, and epušuni or eppušuni. Cf. also, for this infinitive epaše, K. 578: 9, Smith, *Asurb*. III, p. 36 and for the Pret. or Pres. e-pa-šu, Ašurn. Mon., l. 55, e-pa-šu-ni, K. 657: rev. 9, *LK*. 102; cf. also, e-pa-aš, K. 686: 12, *LK*. 173; K. 577: 18, *LK*. 203; K. 657: rev. 6, *LK*. 102, and ip-pa-aš, K. 617: rev. 22, *LK*. 208. Instead of erub. I., 1. Pret. we have e-ra-ab, K. 113: rev. 2, *LK*. 183; e-ra-bu-u-nu, K. 5488: 4, *LK*. 129. Instead of išpur I., 1, Pret., we have liš-pa-ru-u-ni, K. 1013: rev. 16, *LK*. 170, iš-pa-ru-niš-šu, K. 530: 21, *LK*. 158. It is noticeable that the examples given show a predominance of *a* instead of the usual *u*. For a different vocalization, in other places, in verbal forms cf. the following: instead of idabub, or idibub, I., 1. Pres., we have frequently idubub; cf. i-du-bu-bu, K. 625: rev. 8, *LK*. 131; id-du-bu-ub, K. 530: 14, *LK*. 158; ad-du-bu-ub, K. 617: 13, *LK*. 208; for ittadin, I., 2. ittidin, cf. in various forms, K. 112: rev. 2, *LK*. 223; K. 582: rev. 6, *LK*. 167; K. 619: 12, *LK*. 174; K. 541: rev. 3, *LK*. 207, etc. Many other examples of both these classes could be given. In connection with them, cf. Bezold, *Orient. Dipl*. p. XXXVI.

R^M 2, 2.

OBVERSE.—l. 1. duppu. Very few letters begin in any but the stereotyped way, which is so familiar that it need not be mentioned. This is one of the most informal, not to say brusque. The beginning with duppu is found in but few letters.[1] It would seem that there was some special reason for its employment. That of Bezold[2] seems very probable, that it was the way in which the scribes, who arranged the letters in the royal libraries, commenced those of which the beginning had been lost, or badly mutilated. A fact tending to confirm this view is that duppu here is followed by the expression a-na-ka, instead of the almost universal third person, and in K. 1396 duppu is followed in the same way by a-na ka-a-si.

l. 2. ^amêlu nâgir bîti. Cf. ^amêlu nâgir ekalli, K. 485: 1, *LK.* 112.

l. 3. a-na-ka. The independent form of the pronoun is generally used, with the ordinary prepositions, including ana.[3] With some longer prepositions the suffix is used, thus with muḫḫi, panatu, maḫri, libbi, battubatti,[4] etc. The use here of a-na-ka is exceptional.

l. 5. It is a peculiarity very characteristic of the letters that the ending a-a, which is properly the Gentilic ending, has become commonly used with ordinary names of cities and countries. This usage is so very common that examples need not be given.

l. 6. e-muḳ-ḳi-šu, *his soldiers.* The writing e-muḳ-ḳi, instead of e-mu-ḳi, is quite common.

l. 7. kar-ka-te-e. Cf. *AV.* 4208. I think it is certainly to be read as one word and is an adjective modifying emuḳê. Its meaning would then be something like *strong, mighty.* U-a-si occurs in the same form in l. 14 and in the form U-e-si, an interesting variation, in R^m 2, 3: rev. 6. Both forms occur elsewhere.[5]

l. 10. ḳa-ni. This passage is quoted by Delitzsch in the passage above cited.

l. 15. uḫ-ḫu-ru. From root אחר₁, used often as a technical astronomical term; cf. Del. *HWB.* p. 44, Jensen, *Kosmologie.* It has a non-technical use, however, as is evident from this passage. This letter is not dealing with astronomy, or astrology. Its natural meaning would be, *to be behind, to delay.* This is preterite, instead of the usual uḫḫir, and ilakûni follows it in the present. It is then to be translated, "the prefects have delayed in going." It may, however, have a semi-technical meaning, "took observations."

---

[1] Cf. K. 1396, *LK.* 185; K. 831, *LK.* 214; K. 1239, *LK.* 219.

[2] *Die Thontafelsammlungen des British Museum,* p. 17.

[3] Cf. *DG.*, p. 131, § 55, 1 b).

[4] Cf. *DG.*, § 81, b).

[5] Cf. U-a-a-si; K. 5464: 27 and probably rev. 4, *LK.* 198. U-e-si, K. 5464: rev. 2. Cf. also *PSBA.*, Nov. 5, 1895, 234. K. 5464 presents an interesting parallel with the present letter on several other points.

REVERSE.—l. 4. ša la pi-i. Cf. K. 1187 : 5, *LK.* 217. Literally, *what is not the mouth of the king my lord*,=" what the king my lord has not commanded."

l. 6. ti is probably to be supplied, as omitted by the carelessness of the scribe.

l. 7. lu la. An emphatic negative. Not common, but occurring several times in the letters. me-me-ni..........lâ form a usual combination, = "*not at all.*" Cf. *BAS.*, I., 1., p. 217.

l. 9. ak-tal-šu-u from kalû. Cf. *DG.*, §39.

l. 11. a-ki-e. Probably equivalent to a-ki-i preposition or conjunction, meaning *as.* Cf. *HWB.*, p. 52.

R^{M} 2, 3.

OBVERSE.—l. 4. The use of determinatives here is a question which admits of discussion. Bezold claims[1] in a case similar, but without the amêlu, that ṣâbê is a determinative. The use of amêlu here renders that supposition improbable. In R^{m} 2, 7 : 5 there is more probability that the ṣâbê is a determinative.

l. 8. u-ta-me-šu. II., 2, from נמשׁ, the root from which attumuš is the most common form. This root occurs quite frequently in the letters.[2] The meaning *set out, depart*, usually given to attumuš, suits all the cases. A recognition of this root, outside of the form attumuš permits the correction of Delitzsch's transliteration and translation in two letters. Thus in K. 526 : 14, I read u-ta-miš-u-ni instead of his u-ta-rid-u-ni[3], giving a much better meaning, and showing the same form which occurs in our present letter. Again in K. 146 : 10, *LK.* 192, instead of Delitzsch's difficult šam-na mu-šu,[4] I read u-na-mu-šu, making that part of the letter perfectly clear, with the following translation for ls. 9 and 10, *the twenty-eighth day they remained there, on the twenty-ninth day they* (or *I*) *departed.* The form in this last case is unammuš, where usually we have unammaš, but this variation is sufficiently common to cause trouble. S. A. Smith and Strassmaier (cf. references quoted by Delitzsch) had no doubt given the correct transliteration, but had failed to give the right connection of words and interpretation.

l. 9. a-ṣa-ap-pu-šu. Some animal, evidently an animal for riding, probably some kind of horse. I read with *p* rather than *b* on account of R^{m} 2, 8 : rev. 1, where .... ṣap-pa is preceded and followed by bit-ḫal-li, and is probably the same word as this. A-zap-pu would be equally good.

---

[1] Cf. *Or. Dipl.* XVI. § 7. (c).

[2] Besides the forms given in the glossary to these letters, cf. u-na-maš-u-ni K. 1170 : 10, 11, *LK.* 147; and u-ta-me-ši, K. 621, 14 (unpublished); cf, also, *BOD.*, p. 101.

[3] Cf. *BAS.*, I., 1, p. 203-4. Here S. A. Smith had previously read u-ta-lak-u-ni, *Assyrian Letters*, part III., p. 23.

[4] Cf. *BAS.*, I., 1, p. 204-5.

REVERSE.—l. 7. u-di-na. I accept here the meaning given by Johns,[1] *as yet*, with negative, *not yet*. I would connect it closely with Heb. עוֹד, at which derivation he only hints. The ending is the adverbial ending.

R^{M} 2, 4.

OBVERSE.—l. 6. da-gil-iṣṣurê pl.. For the form as a compound word, cf. Del. *BAS.*, I., 1, p. 219. K. 572 : 9, *LK.* 23, shows that this was a regular court officer, and that the whole word is plural. That it means a diviner is self-evident. Our word augur, the Latin *augur*, and the Greek οἰωνόμαντις testify to the same custom among the Romans and Greeks.

l. 10. lu-uk-ta-ti-ni, is probably from the root kênu (כון) *to stand.* Such a meaning is required by the context. The stem is افتعل, for which cf. the similar forms given by Bezold[2]; cf. also *DG.* § 83, note.

REVERSE.—l. 3. It is very evident that the signs which I have left untransliterated in ls. 3 and 5 and the whole of l. 6, have been erased. The meaning is complete without them.

l. 5. la i-ši-i. As already noted, this form written separately, is comparatively rare in the letters.

l. 9. ur-ki-ia-u. Cf. Del., *HWB.*, p. 243.

l. 12. am-me-ia-u. Probably equals ammû *this*, the not very common masc. singular of the word frequently occurring in the letters as ammâti in the fem. plur. and ammûte in the masc. pl. This word is much more common than generally supposed. It occurs several times in the Tel el-Amarna tablets.[3] It is very common in the Assyrian letters.[4] I am inclined to favor the view of Bezold that it is simply another form of annû, *n* being changed to *m*.

R^{m} 2, 5.

OBVERSE.—l 8. uṣ-ṣu-ru. A good imperative form. It, however, looks like a plural where a singular is needed. It may possibly be a plural, being a command addressed to the present scribe and those associated with him. It may be an instance of the overhanging vowels which are used in the Letters, in accordance with laws not yet fully determined.

l. 9. mar. Probably an ideogram the reading of which is uncertain. The meaning, however, from this and other passages,[5] is reasonably certain, viz., *time*, with ištu, *from the time that.*

---

1 Cf. *PSBA*, Nov. 5, 1895, 228 sq.

2 Cf. *Or. Dipl.* p. XXXVII, § 29.

3 Cf. *Or. Dipl.* p. XX and 76.

4 Cf. masc. pl. am-mu-te, or am-mu-ti, K. 112: 11, *LK.* 223; K. 1013: rev. 9, *LK.* 170; K. 472: 12, *LK.* 17; K. 490: rev. 7, *LK.* 18. Fem. pl. am-ma-te, or am-ma-ti, K. 662: 13, *LK.* 211, and other examples.

5 For passages in which the same expression occurs cf. K. 653: rev. 10, *LK.* 154, and K. 662: 15, *LK.* 211.

REVERSE.—l. 2. an-nu-ri. An interesting form. From its use, it certainly has the same meaning as annušim. This is shown by the way in which it stands here, preceded by umâ, and by the context in other passages in which it occurs.[1] Two possibilities present themselves. This may be an independent word, possibly related, having the same meaning as annušim; or it may be that we are to give ri a new value šim.

ls. 5–6. The expression used in these two lines seems to be stereotyped; cf. very similar expressions elsewhere.[2]

R^m 2, 6.

REVERSE.—l. 2. Nu-ka-al is found elsewhere. Cf. nu-ka-la, K. 1039 : 11, 12, which is probably from the root kalû (כלה) = *to delay*. This may be a different root.

l. 10. The meaning *either*........*or* has usually been given to lû...... lû. Cf. *DG.* § 82 and Del., *Prol.*, p. 135. It may be questioned, however, whether the meaning *both*........*and* is not more suitable here. Cf. also other places where it is found.[3] A new usage is the expression used in the letters šumma........ šumma, meaning *whether*........*or*.

l. 14. mu-gir-ri. This word is not given in Del. *HWB.* A synonym of narkabtu, as is shown here by the determinative iṣu and by the context. From נגר, *a chariot*, as being that which runs. The form is perhaps مُفْعِل but more probably مَفْعَل with transition of *a* to *i*.

R^m 2, 7.

l. 7. Na-ṣa, occurs in another form in R^m. 2, 11, and R^m. 2, 464, where it will be discussed.

R^m 2, 8.

OBVERSE.—l. 4. a-dan-niš. Entirely untenable are the derivations of Delitzsch from ויאר[4]; of Zimmern, from אדן[5], and of Jensen from ויאר[6], with the meaning, *appointed time*, like Heb. מועד. All these make it an adverbial formation from a noun adannu. It is probably from ana danniš, as given by Harper[7].

[1] Cf. K. 656 : 11, *LK.* 92; K. 175 : 11, *LK.* 221; K. 472 : 7, *LK.* 17. Cf. also, K. 1170 : 9, *LK.* 147, where we have a-nu-su, and the various forms in the Tel el-Amarna tablets: cf. Bezold, *Or. Dipl.*, pp. xl. and 76.

[2] Cf. a-na šul-me ša šarri at-tal-ka, K. 532: rev. 13, 14, *LK.* 109; a-na šul-me ina muḫḫi šar mâtu Akkad-a-a it-tal-ku, *K.* 181: rev. 18-19, *LK.* 197; a-na šul-me ina muḫ-ḫi-šu-ma it-ta-la-ak, K. 181: rev. 21-22, *LK.* 197.

[3] Cf. K. 1306 : 4, *LK.* 185; K. 112 : 6, *LK.* 223.

[4] *HWB.*, p. 26.

[5] *BAS.*, p. 18 note. He compares Heb. אָרוֹן and אֹרֶן, p. 107.

[6] *Kosmologie*, p. 414 sqq.

[7] HEBRAICA, X. 1 and 2, p. 107.

l. 8. The restoration of this and the following lines is taken from similar phrases which occur elsewhere.[1]

ls. 10–12. This restoration is given chiefly from a combination of two passages.[2]

REVERSE.—l. 3. For the reading, cf. K. 582 : 5, *LK.* 167, where the name is also without determinative. The portion of Dûr preserved has the form of narkabtu.

l. 8. For all this passage from Obv. 19 through to the end, cf. K. 1113 and K. 1229, *LK.* 71, by the same scribe, which presents many parallels. The reading of Kur$^{pl.}$ as sisê here and in ls. 10 and 12, while not very frequent, is well authenticated.[3]

l. 8. as-si-kal. For the root, cf. Johns, *PSBA.*, Nov. 5, 1895, p. 234.

l. 10. u-ša-ad-la-ab. Del., *HWB.*, p. 217–8 gives two roots, דלב, neither of which is suitable here. The context, especially ana mîni, indicates the meaning, *reckoned.*

l. 10. la-as-kal. Undoubtedly the same as as-si-kal in l. 8. This may be a case of unusual syncope. It is, however, more in harmony with the usual custom of the letters to consider the sign si as omitted by the carelessness of the scribe.

R^{M} 2, 11.

REVERSE.—l. 2. na-ṣu-ni-šu. This root has been discussed both by S. A. Smith and by Delitzsch.[4] Smith compares both Hebrew נצא and נצה, and thinks that this root combines both their meanings *hinfliehen* and *streiten.* Passages in which it is found in the letters he translates are K. 359 : 5, 10 ; K. 525 : 25 ; K. 582 : 8.

Delitzsch gives as the root נצה. He, however, thinks it combines the meanings *herbeieilen* and *enteilen*, *entfliehen.* In addition to the passages given by Smith, he quotes only K. 186 : 4. Many other examples of its occurrence may be given.[5] A careful comparison of all these makes it probable that the root is נ׳צא. Its meaning is similar to י׳צא, but in some passages like the present is evidently the transitive, *bring out.* The *hapax legomenon* נָצֹא, Jer. 48:9, is to be taken from the same root in Hebrew, if the text of the passage is correct. Johns

---

[1] For nummur cf. the similar phrase in K. 60 1: rev. 12, *LK.* 7.

[2] Cf. K. 627: 9-11, *LK.* 115 and K. 499: 9–10, *LK.* 119.

[3] Cf. K. 1113: 7 sqq. and note of Del., *BAS.* II. 1., pp. 45–6.

[4] For S. A. Smith, cf. *Die Keilschrifttexte Asurbanipals*, part II., p. 53. For Delitzsch, *BAS.*, II., 1, p. 61.

[5] Cf. K. 125: 9, 11, 19, *LK.* 196; K. 181, rev. 28, *LK.* 197; K. 5464: rev. 19, *LK.* 198; K. 186: 4, *LK.* 222; K. 594: rev. 9, *LK.* 90; K. 686: 7, *LK.* 173; K. 582: 8, *LK.* 167; K. 619: rev. 13, *LK.* 174; K. 1461: 15, *LK.* 120; K. 594: rev. 9, *LK.* 90.

has given the meaning *bring*, *PSBA.*, Nov. 5, 1895, 225, 233, 236 sq. but without comment.

It is to be noticed that נשׂא in every case cited is found in the I., 1 perm. with the meaning of the pret. This is one illustration of the fact which has already been noticed,[1] of the more frequent and varied use of the permansive in the letters than in other inscriptions. Other permansives in connection with preterites occur in the letters.[2]

R^M 2, 458.

Letters of the same scribe are found in *LK.* 87-99. Cf. also *BAS.*, II., 1, p. 32 sqq. They show marked similarities. Ašur and Bêltu are the gods invoked in all. This letter down to the middle of line 9 is exactly duplicated in K. 656:1-8, *LK.* 92, and with but slight variation in K. 5466:1-4, *LK.* 99. K. 656 also presents a marked resemblance in subject matter to the present one.

l. 4. For the correctness of the reading ekurrâte, cf. the interesting writing e-kur-ra-a-te, K. 1062:7, *LK.* 216.

R^M. 2, 459.

The general subject of this letter is evidently similar to the preceding. l. 7 bears a marked resemblance to R^m 2, 11:2 and suggests the possibility that they may have the same author.

R^M 2, 462.

l. 2. For another letter by a scribe with the same name, cf. K. 525.[3]

l. 3. This is an unusual use of ištu, where we usually have ina. It is, however, simply a loose use of the ideogram for ištu for other prepositions, such as we have elsewhere, most frequently in Ašurnaṣirpal.[4] The name of this man is interesting. *A father he did not know*, is apparently the meaning.

R^M 2, 463.

l. 9. šup-ru. Evidently imperative. Apparently singular, since the letter is from one man, and in the next word he makes answer in the sing. The *u* at the end may be a supernumerary vowel, as in cases previously mentioned.

R^M 2, 464.

OBVERSE.—l. 5. That a plural sign is to be read in the break is rendered probable by the context, especially bat-te-bat-te-e-a *round about me.* This

---

[1] *ZA.*, V. 1890, pp. 13-21.
[2] Cf. K. 1026: 7, *LK.* 118.
[3] Cf. *BAS.*, II., 1, p. 55, sq.
[4] Cf. Col. 2: 124 (for itti), Col. 3: 39 (for ina).

word might possibly be read ḳêpâni, as Delitzsch has done;[1] but the reading I have given is the standard one. Its occurrence in the letters is certain.[2]

l. 6. A supernumerary vowel between a word, especially preposition and suffix, as here, is common in the letters.[3] Its significance is doubtful. It may mark a change of tone to that syllable.

l. 7. i-sa-al-lu is probably plural, the subject being ḫazânâte. šulmu išâlû = *they ask peace*, i. e. send greeting.

l. 10. ḳa-ra-bu. I think there is no doubt that this is to be considered a perm., as previously remarked. i-sa-ḫa is probably pres. from סחה, *to rebel, revolt.*

l. 11. u-pu-šu. Probably a I. 1. pret., first person. The *u* for *e* is not surprising in the letters. The same form is found elsewhere.[4] A general meaning, *I attended to the matter*, may be given here.

l. 14. pa-tu-u-ni. Evidently from פתא, perm. Its reference may be either to the man Uppiti or the city Uriaku.

l. 16. i-ḳa-bu-u-ni. This is evidently a pres., but it seems to have the force of the pret., because in expressions similar to this the pret. is the form regularly used.

REVERSE.—l. 4. I am inclined to read [ilu] Nabû-emur-an-ni, the sign ŠI being omitted by the scribe, or LAL itself having the ideographic value amâru; cf. the names, Šamaš-emur-an-ni, and Bêl-emur-an-ni.

GLOSSARY.

u, *and*, 1: rev. 21; 2: rev. 11; 6: 4; 7: 9; 11: rev. 7.

abâru (אבר), *to cross.* I. 2. e-tab-ru, 3: 9.

adi (א), *as far as, until.* a-di 1: 20, rev. 1, 8; 2: 6. a-du, *till*, 459: 8.

edu (אד), *one.* edumânu, *alone(?)*, e-du-ma-nu, 11: 10.

u-di-na (אוד), *as yet*, 3: rev. 7.

aḫu (אחה), *brother.* aḫi-šu, 11: 9. aḫi-ka, 11: rev. 3.

aḫiš, *together*, a-ḫi-ia-ši, 1: rev. 14; a-ḫa-ia-ši, 464: 11.

a-ḫu-lam-ma, *on that side*, 6: rev. 11.

aḫâru (אחר), *to be behind.* II. 1. uḫ-ḫu-ru, 2: 15.

âka, *where?* a-a-ka, 2: 8.

---

[1] In K. 507: 13, *LK.* 88, cf. *BAS.*, II., 1. p. 36.

[2] Cf. the writing ḫa-za-nu, in K. 679: 4, *LK.* 212.

[3] Cf. i-si-e-šu, K. 5464: 31, *LK.* 198; i-si-e-a, K. 83b: rev. 16, *LK.* 168; e-mu-ḳi-e-šu, K. 5464: 28, 29, *LK.* 198; K. 181: rev. 11, *LK.* 197; bêl-piḫa-te-e-šu, K. 5464: 14, *LK.* 198; without suffix, cf. a-bi-te-e, K. 939a: 14, *LK.* 46, and many other cases. Cf. also Bezold, *Oriental Diplomacy*, p. XXIII.

[4] Cf. Ašurnaṣirpal, Col. 3: 125; K. 515: rev. 14, *LK.* 89.

akî (א$_1$), *as, like.* a-ki, 4: rev. 7. a-ki-e, 2: rev. 11.

ekallu, *palace.* ekalli, 5: rev. 6.

ekurru, *temple.* ekurrâte$^{pl.}$ (E-KUR$^{pl.}$) 458: 4.

ilu (אל$_1$), *God.* ilu, determ. 6: 4^2; 8: 5^2, 7^3; 458: 8^2; 459: 4^2. ili, 6: rev. 10.

alu, *city.* alu, determ. 1: 5, 8, 11, 12, 15, 16, 18, 20, 23, rev. 5, 8, 9, 13, 26, 31; 2: 9, 14, rev. 1; 3: 7, rev. 6; 7: 7; 11: 6; 458: 5; 463: 4, 8; 464: 3, 9, 13, rev. 9. ali-šu, 11: 7.

ûlâ (אולי$_1$), *perhaps.* u-la, 6: 7.

a-li-e, *where?* 11: rev. 3.

elû (אלה$_4$), *to be high.* III. 2. u-se-li, 1: rev. 29.

alâku (אלך$_2$), *to go.* I. 1. Pret. i-li-kan-a-ni, 1: 8, 21. i-lik-an-ni, 2: rev. 9. il-li-kam-ma, 11: rev. 4. al-lik-an-ni, 464: rev. 2. I. 1. Pres. i-lak, 2: 7, 14. i-la-ku-u-ni, 2: 15. il-lak, 3: rev. 7. il-la-ka, 5: rev. 4. al-lak, 5: rev. 6. I. 2. i-ta-lak, 1: 13. i-tal-ku-u-ni, 2: 11. it-tal-ku, 11: 7.

ellu (אלל$_2$) *bright,* 3: 7.

umâ, *now.* u-ma-a, 1: 21; 4: rev. 7; 5: rev. 1.

amêlu (אמל), *officer,* determ. 1: 7, rev. 15, 17, 18, 22, 25, 27, 30^2; 2: 2, 6, 9, 10, 15; 3: 4, 5^2, 6, 13, rev. 2; 4: 5, 6, 12, rev. 9; 5: 5; 6: 14, rev. 9, 11; 11: rev. 7; 462: 5; 463: 6, 7, 10^2; 464: 5, 11, 13, rev. 4, 7; a-me-li, 6: 8.

am-me-ia-u, *this,* 4: rev. 12.

umâmu (אמם), *beast.* u-ma-me, 1: rev. 9.

ummânu, *people.* u-ma-ni-e, 458: rev. 3.

emêḳu (אמק$_4$), *to be deep.* emûḳu, *warriors.* ^{amêlu} e-muḳ-ḳi-šu, 2: 6.

amâru (אמר$_1$), *to see.* I. 1. e-mu-ru-šu, 11: 5.

imêru (אמר$_3$), *animal,* determ. 1: 9, 11, 16, 19, 24; 3: 9.

ina, *in.* ina, 1: 4, 10, 11, 12, 19, 23, 24, rev. 6, 13, 15, 17, 18, 28, 31; 2: 12, 14, rev. 1, 6; 3: 11, rev. 6; 4: 5, 9, rev. 10; 5: 4, rev. 6; 6: 7, 9, 10; 7: 7; 11: 4, 7, 10, rev. 4, 8; 458: 9; 459: 5; 463: 8; 464: 2, 7, 9, 12, rev. 1, 8, 10. i-[na], 1: 9.

ana, *to.* a-na, 1: 1, 3, 8, 13, 20, rev. 9; 2: 2; 3: 1, 3, 7; 4: 1, 4, rev. 13; 5: 1, 3, rev. 5; 6: 1, 3, 5, rev. 1, 3; 7: 1, 3; 8: 1, 3, 6, 15, 16, 17, rev. 9; 11: 6; 458: 1, 3, 4, 5, 6, 7, 8; 459: [1], 3, 4; 462: [1], 3; 463: 1, 3, 4; 464: 4, 15, rev. 3, 9, 13. a-na-ka, 2: 3.

an-ni-u, *this,* 2: rev. 11; 6: rev. 7; 8: rev. 4. an-ni-[u], 8: rev. 6.

anâku (אנך$_1$), *I.* a-na-ku, 1: 23; 464: rev. 1, 9.

an-nu-ri, *just now,* 5: rev. 2.

annûšim, *just now.* a-nu-šim, 1, rev. 30; an-nu-šim, 11: rev. 5.

is-si-e-šu (א$_1$), *with him,* 464: rev. 8.

epêšu (אפשׁ) *to do, make.* I. 1. e-pu-šu, 2: 12, rev. 2. e-pu-šu-ni, 2: rev. 10. [e]-pu-šu, 8: rev. 6. u-pu-šu, 464: 11. I. 2. e-tap-ša, 2: rev. 10.

iṣu (אץ), *tree.* iṣu, determ. 1: rev. 6; 6: 9, rev. 4, 14; 458: 9, rev. 4; 459: 5.

aṣappu, probably some kind of horse. imêru a-ṣap-pu-šu, 3: 9; [a]-ṣap-pa, 8: rev. 1.

erêbu (ארב), *to enter.* I. 1. e-ru-bu-u-ni, 464: rev. 10. I. 2. e-tar-bu-u-ni, 8: rev. 5.

ardu, *servant.* ardu-ka, 1: 2; 3: 2; 4: 2; 5: 2; 6: 2; 7: 2; 8: 2; 458: 2; 459: 2; 462: 2; 463: 2.

urû (ארה), *stall.* u-ru-u, 1: 15, 16.

aširti (bît ali), *sanctuary,* 2: 12.

ištu, *from.* ištu, 1: 5, 7, 18, rev. 8; 4: 6, 12, rev. 4; 5: 9; 6: rev. 3; 7: 12; 462: 4.

itti (א), *with.* it-[ti]-šu, 2: rev. 6.

atâ (אתה), *now.* a-ta-a, 1: 6; 6: rev. 12.

etêḳu (אתק), *to march.* I. 1. e-ti-iḳ, 6: 8. I. 2. i-ta-ta-ka, 4: rev. 14.

i-tu-uḳ-tu, 1: rev. 19.

---

bîtu (בית), *house.* bît, 1: rev. 27, 30.

bêlu (באל), *lord.* be-ili (*my lord,* nom). 1: 4, 14, 22, rev. 4, 10, 16, 21, 31; 4: 7; 5: 6, 9; 8: rev. 11, 13; 11: 1; 459: 6, 8; 463: 5. bêli (*my lord,* nom.) 4: rev. 8; 462: 6. be-li (*my lord,* nom.) 6: 6, 11, rev. 6. bêli-ia (*my lord,* gen.) 1: 1, 3, rev. 31; 4: 1, 4; 6: 1, 3, 5, rev. 15; 458: 1, 7, 8, rev. 5; 459: 1, 3, [4]; 463: 3. bêli-a (gen.) 5: 1, 3; 11: rev. 5; 462: [1], 3; 464: 15. be-ili-ia (gen.) 3; [1], 3; 8: 1, 3, 6, 9, [11], [12]; 463: 1. be-ili-a, 1: rev. 10 and 11. amêlu bêl piḫâti, *prefect.* 2: 9, 10; 3: 6, 13. amêlu bêl piḫâtê pl., 2: 15.

bi-rit, *among, between,* 6: 7, 15.

bid, *as, when.* bid, 1: 22.

bitḫallu, *riding horse.* bit-ḫal-li, 8: 19, rev. 2.

bat-te-bat-te-e-a, *round about me,* 464: 6.

---

garâru (גרר), *to run.* iṣu mu-gir-ri, *chariot,* 6: rev. 14.

gušûru (גשׁר), *beam.* (iṣu) gušûrê pl., 458: 9, rev. 4; 459: [5].

---

dabâbu (דבב), *to speak.* I. 1. Pres. i-da-bu-ub, 2: 13; id-da-ab, 7: 10.

dâgil-iṣṣûri, *bird inspector, augur.* amêlu da-gil-iṣṣûrê pl., 4: 6, 12.

dâku (דוך), *to kill.* I. 1. i-du-u-ku, 464: 12.

dalâbu (דלב), *to reckon(?)* III. 1. u-ša-ad-la-ab, 8: rev. 10.

dul-lu, *business,* 2: 11, rev. 2. dul-li, 2: rev. 6.

a-dan-niš (דנן) *very much,* 8: 4², 458: rev. 2.

duppu, *tablet.* duppu, 2: 1.

---

abâlu (ובל), *to bring.* I. 1. Pres. u-bal-u-ni-šu-nu, 1: rev. 30. u-ba-la, 2: rev. 7. I. 1. Pret. lu-u-bi-lu-ni-šu, 11: 3. III. 1. Impv. še-bi-la, 464: rev. 12.

adû (ודה), *appoint.* I. 1. u-da, 1: rev. 4. tu-da, 1: rev. 23.

aṣû (וצא), *to go out.* I. 1. tu-ṣu-u-ni, 6: 10. I. 2. i-tu-ṣi, 1: 18. II. 2. u-ta-ṣi-ṣi, 1: rev. 20; u-ta-ṣi 4: rev. 2. ṣêtu, *end.* ṣa-at, 8: 17.

ašâbu (ושב), *to dwell.* I. 1. Pres. u-šab, 2: 8, 14.

urkîu (ורך), *later.* ur-ki-ia-u, 4: rev. 9.

---

zammêru, *singer.* amêlu zammêrê pl. 1: rev. 15, 22, 30.

zêru (זרא), *seed, family.* zi-ri-ka, 8: 16.

ḫazânu, *mayor of city.* amêlu ḫazânu (bêl ali), 464: 5, 13.

ḫalâḳu (חלק), *to flee.* I. 2. iḫ-tal-ḳa, 464: rev. 3.

ṭêmu (טאם), *tidings.* ṭe-mu, 1: rev. 11. ṭe-[e-mu], 464: 7.

ṭâbu (טוב), *to be good.* I. 1. Perm. ṭâb, 458: rev. 6.

---

iaši, *I.* ia-ši, 464: 10.

ûmu (יום), *day.* ûme (UD-ME) 8: 17. ûmu (UD-MU) 8: rev. 4; 464: rev. 8. ûmi (UD), 8: rev. 15; 464: 2.

išû (ישה), *to be.* I. 1. i-šu-u-ni, 4: 13. i-ši-i, 4: rev. 5; contracted with lâ to lâšû; la-šu, 1: 6, rev. 20; la-a-šu, 11: 5; la-a-aš-šu, 11: 8.

---

imêru ku-din, *mule,* 1: 9, 11, 16, 19, 24.

kânu (כון), *to be firm.* II. 1. lu-ki-in-nu, 8: 12. II. 2. lu-uk-ta-ti-ni, 4: 10. ki-e-ni, *firm,* 8: 13.

kî (כי), *when.* ki-i, 1: 7, 21, rev. 5, 24; 2: rev. 8; 464: rev. 1.

ki, determ. 2: rev. 8; 7: 6; 458: 3, 6.

kalû (כלא), *to delay, restrain, imprison.* I. 2. ak-ta-la, 4: rev. 11; ak-tal-šu-u, 2: rev. 9.

kîlu (כלא), *prison, restraint.* kil-la-šu, 2: rev. 12.

kaliu, *impedimenta.* ka-li-ia, 1: 4. ka-li-ia-u, 1: 6, 19, rev. 12. ka-li-e, 1: 20.

kîma, *like.* ki-ma, 6: 13; 464: rev. 12.

ka-a-a-ma-ni-u, *continual,* 8: rev. 9.

kamûtu (כמה), *captivity.* kam-mu-su, 11: rev. 1.

kanâšu (כנש), *to submit.* I, 1. Pres. i-ka-an-nu-šu, 6: rev. 16.

karâbu (כרב), *to bless.* lik-ru-bu, 6: 5; 8: 6; 458: 9; 459: 5.

kar-ka-te-e, *mighty* (?) 2: 7.

karâru (כרר), *to be situated.* I. 1. Perm. ka-ri-ru-u-ni, 1: rev. 7.

kiššatu (כשש), *totality.* kiššat, 6: rev. 10[2].

---

lâ (לא), *not.* la, 1: rev. 21; 2: rev. 4, 7; 3: rev. 8; 4: rev. 5; 6: rev. 13, 16; 11: rev. 4; 463: 12, 13. la-a, 11: 5; 459: 8.

libbu (לבב), *heart, midst.* lib-bu, 458: rev. 5. libbi, 1: rev. 6, 28; 3: rev. 6; 11: 7; 463: 11; 464: rev. 8. lib-bi, 11: 10.

lû (לו), *surely.* lu 1: 3, rev. 23; 2: 3, rev. 7; 3: 3; 5: 3; 6: 3; 7: 3; 8: 3; 458: 7; 459: 3. lu-u, 4: 3; 458: rev. 6; 462: 3; 463: 3. lu-u......... lu-u, *both....and,* 6: rev. 10.

lîpu, *descendant.* li-pi-i-ka, 8: 15.

---

mâ, *saying.* ma-a, 1: 6, rev. 17, 22, 23; 2: 5, 8, 13, 15, rev. 4; 3: rev. 5; 4: 9, 11; 5: 7, rev. 5; 6: 7, 12; 7: 11; 11: 2, rev. 4; 459: 7; 462: 7; 463: 6.

mâdu (מאד), *much.* ma-a-du, 458: rev. 4.

mâru (מאר), *child, son.* amêlu mârâ pl.-ni, 1: rev. 17. amêlu mârâni pl.-šu, 464: rev. 7.

nâru ME. 3: 8.

mûšu (מוש), *night.* mu-šu, 8: rev. 6.

muḫḫi, *above, upon, with reference to.* muḫḫi, 1: 4, rev. 15, 17; 4: 5; 5: 4; 6: 9; 11: rev. 8; 458: 9; 459: 5; 462: 4; 464: 7, 12, rev. 10. muḫ-ḫi-šu, 6: 10. muḫ-ḫi-a, 11: rev. 4.

mala, *as many as.* ma-la, 1: 14; 3: 10. (Both doubtful because of breaks.)

manû (מנה), *to number.* mi-i-ni, *number,* 8: rev. 9.

mînu (with ša), *according as.* me-i-nu(ša), 4: 11; mi-i-nu(ša), 8: rev. 13. memeni, *at all.* me-me-ni, 4: rev. 3.

maṣû (מצה ?), *to be wide, sufficient.* III. 1. Perm. šum-ṣa, 1: rev. 28.

MAR, *time?* 5: 9.

mâtu, *land.* mâtu, determ. 1: 13, rev. 18; 2: 5, 10, rev. 8; 3: rev. 1; 7: 6; 11: 4; 458: 6; 462: 5; 464: rev. 3. mât-su, 6: rev. 10.

---

nâru (נאר), *river.* nâru, determ. 3: 8.

amêlu NA. 464: rev. 4.

amêlu nâgir ekalli, *overseer of the palace,* 1: rev. 27. amêlu nâgir bîti, *overseer of the house,* 2: 2.

nadânu (נדן), *to give.* I. 1. [li]d-din, 4: 15. [lid-di]-nu, 8: 18; ta-da-in, *gift(?)* 1: rev. 10.

nazâzu (נזז), *to stand.* III. 1. u-ša-zi-zu-u-ni, 1: 17. lu-ša-zi-zu, 1: rev. 14.

nuk, *saying.* nu-uk, 11: rev. 3.

nu-ka-al, 6: rev. 2.

nakâru (נכר), *to be hostile.* I. 1. part. nak-ru-ti-šu-nu, 6: rev. 13.

namâšu (נמש), *to set out, depart.* II. 1. u-nam-maš, 3: rev. 8. II. 2. u-ta-me-šu, 3: 8; u-tam-me-ša, 5: rev. 3; u-ta-mi-šu-ma, 3: rev. 3.

naṣû (נצא), *to bring out.* I. 1. Perm. na-ṣa, 7: 7; na-ṣu-ni-šu, 11: rev. 2; na-ṣu-u-ni, 464: rev. 13.

naṣaru (נצר), *to save.* I. 1. Pres. i-na-ṣur, 1: rev. 29. I. 1. Pret. li-iṣ-ṣu-ru, 8: 9. I. 1. Impv. uṣ-ṣu-ru, 5: 8. I. 2. Pret. it-ta-aṣ-ru, 5: 13. maṣṣartu, *watch.* maṣṣarti-šu, 4: rev. 13. ma-ṣar-tu-šu, 5: 8, 11. maṣṣarâti pl., 464: 4.

nu-ti-in, 1: rev. 15.

---

saḫû (סחה), *to rebel.* I. 1. i-sa-ḫa, 464: 10.

saḫâru (סחר), *to turn.* I. 2. lu-u-sa-ḫi-ri, 4: 14.

sisû, *horse.* sisê pl. 8: rev. 8, 10, 12.

---

pû (פו), *mouth.* pi-i, 2: rev. 4.

iṣu pi-lu-ur-te, 1: rev. 6.

pânu (פנה), *before.* pân 1: rev. 31; 4: 12. pâni-ka, 4: 9. pa-ni-šu, 3: 11. pa-ni-šu-nu, 4: rev. 4. pâni-šu-nu, 4: rev. 10. pânâtu, *before.* pa-na-tu-šu-nu, 1: 9. pa-ni-tu, 464: rev. 1.

pu-ri-di, 6: 7, 12, 13, rev. 5.

pâriṣu (פרץ), *judge.* amêlu pa-ri-ṣu-u-te, 1: rev. 25.

pu-tu, *side, entrance,* 3: 7. pu-ut, 3: rev. 1.

patû (פתא), *to open.* I. 1. ap-ta, 1: rev. 24; Perm. pa-tu-u-ni; 464: 14.

paḫâru (פחר), *to collect.* II. 2. up-ta-at-ḫu-ru, 1: rev. 28.

ṣâbu (צבא), *soldier.* amêlu ṣâbê pl., 3: 4; 7: 5, 9; 463: 10; 464: 11. amêlu ṣâbê pl.-šu, 3: rev. 2.

ṣabâtu (צבת), *seize, take.* I. 1. i-ṣa-bat, 1: 11; i-ṣab-tu, 11: 11; iṣ-ṣab-tu-ni-šu, 464: rev. 7. II. 1. tu-ṣa-bit, 1: rev. 23; u-ṣa-bit-u-ni, 1: rev. 29.

_____

ḳibû (קבא), *to speak, command.* I. 1. Pret. iḳ-bu-u-ni, 4: rev. 8; ni-iḳ-bi, 6: rev. 12. I. 1. Pres. i-ḳab-[bi], 6: 11; i-ḳab-bi, 8: rev. 11; a-ḳa-bu-u-ni, 464: 16. ḳu-bu, *cry*, 1: rev. 28.
ḳâtu, *hand.* ḳa-ti, 5: 7, 12.
ḳanu (probably), *side, border.* ḳa-an-ni, 1: rev. 31. ḳa-ni, 2: 10.
ḳarâbu (קרב), *to be near.* I. 1. Perm. ḳa-ra-bu, 464: 10.
ḳitridu (קרד), *mighty one*, 6: rev. 9.

_____

amêlu rab-bi-LUL, *music director*, 463: 10.
amêlu rab-SE-ŠA, *chief of the sacrificial festivity*, 1: rev. 18.
amêlu rab-šabrê ᵖˡ·, *chief of the magicians*, 3: 5.
mardîtu (רדה), *road.* mar-di-tu, 1: rev. 7.
narkabtu (רכב), *chariot.* iṣu narkabt-e, 6: 9. iṣu narkabti, 6: rev. 4.
rakâsu (רכס) *to bind.* I. 2. ar-ta-kas, 1: 10, 25. ir-ta-kas, 1: 12.

_____

ša, *which;* has also the force and meaning *of.* ša, *which*, 1: 4, rev. 16; 2: 4, rev. 3, 4, 10; 3: 12; 4: 6, 7; 5: 6; 6: 6, 9, 14, rev. 6; 8: rev. 7; 11: 1; 458: 10; 459: 6; 462: 6; 463: 5, 11; 464: 6, 11, 14, 15, rev. 9. ša, *of*, 1: 15, 16, rev. 18, 26, 27, 30, 31; 2: 9, 10, rev. 5; 3: 6, 7, 10, rev. 1; 6: rev. 5, 15; 8: 8, 10, rev. 10; 458: rev. 5; 463: 10; 464: 2, 8, 13, rev. 5.
šû = *he.* šu-u, 3: 11; 6: 15, rev. 2.
ša'âlu (שׁאל), *to ask.* I. 2. a-sa-al, 1: rev. 19. a-sa-'a-la, 4: rev. 1. a-sa-[al], 11: 3. a-sa-al-šu, 11: rev. 2. i-sa-al-lu, 464: 7.
šadâdu (שׁדד), *to draw.* I. 1. liš-da-du, 459: 7.
šakâlu (שׁכל), *to care for.* I. 2. as-si-kal, 8: rev. 8. la-as-kal, 8: rev. 12.
šêpu, *foot.* šêpâ ᵖˡ·, 3: 4.
šakânu (שׁכן), *to establish.* I. 1. Perm. ši-ku-n, 1: rev. 11. amêlu šakan-maṣṣarti, *commander of the watch*, 4: 5, rev. 9.
šalâmu (שׁלם), *to complete.* II. 1. tu-šal-lum-ni, 1: rev. 24. šulmu, *peace.* šul-mu, 1: 3; 2: 3; 3: 3; 4: 3; 5: 3; 6: 3; 7: 3; 8: 3; 458: 3, 4, 5, 6, 7; 459: 3; 462: 3; 463: 3, 4; 464: 5, 6. šul-me, 5: rev. 5.
šum-ku-un(?), *your name*, 464: rev. 11.
šemû (שׁמא), *to hear.* I. 1. Pret. ni-iš-me, 1: rev. 21. I. 2. Pret. a-si-me, 3: rev. 5. i-si-me, 464: rev. 5.
šumma, *if.* šum-ma, 1: rev. 22, 29; 8: rev. 11.
*6

amêlu ša-nu-te, *second officer*, 3: 5.

šattu (שנה), *year*. šanâti^pl. (MU-AN-NA^pl.) 8: 11.

šapâlu (שפל), *to be low*. šaplu, *under*. šapli (KI-TA), 1: 10, 12, 24. šapli-šu (KI-TA), 1: 19. šap-li, 5: 7. šap-la, 5: 12; 6: 9, rev. 4, 14.

šapâru (שפר), *to send*. I. 1. iš-pur-an-ni, 1: 5, rev. 16; 4: 8; 5: 6, 10; 6: 6; 458: 10; 459: 6; 462: 6; 463: 5. taš-pur-an-ni, 2: 4, rev. 3. iš-pur-šu-u-ni, 1: 22; i-šap-ra, 1: rev. 22. a-šap-ra, 463: 9; i-šap-par-an-ni, 8: rev. 14; liš-pa-r[u], 463; rev. 2. Impv. šu-pur, 11: 2; 459: 7. šup-ru, 463: 9. I. 2. i-sa-ap-ru, 464: rev. 6; a-sa-par, 5: 11; a-sa-ap-ra, 464: rev. 11.

šarru (שרר), *king*. šarru, 1: 4, 14, 22, rev. 4, 10, 16, 21, 31; 2: 13; 3: rev. 5; 4: 7, rev. 7; 5: 6, 9; 6: 6, 11, rev. 6; 8: rev. 11, 13; 11: 1; 458: 10; 459: 6, 8; 462: 6; 463: 5. šar, 2: 5. rev. 8. šarri, 1: 1, 3, rev. 31; 2: rev. 5; 3: 1, 3; 4: 1, 4; 5: 1, 3; 6: 1, 3, 5, rev. 10, 15; 7: 1, 3; 8: 1, 3, 6, 8, 10, rev. 10; 11: rev. 5; 458: 1, 7, 8, rev. 5; 459: 1, 3, 4; 462: [1], 3; 463: 1, 3; 464: 15, rev. 5. šarrâni ^pl., 6: rev. 13. šar-ru-u-tu, *royalty*, 8: 14.

šu-u-tu, *that, the aforesaid*, 11: 9; 464: 8, rev. 2, 5.

---

tebû (תבא), *enemy*. tebê^pl., 7: 5.

mutîr puti, *body guard*. amêlu mutîr pu-te, 1: 7; 7: 4; 462: 5.

ti-[ma]-a-li (תמל), *yesterday*, 8: rev. 7.

The following numerals occur in these letters, written in each case without any phonetic complement.

2. 1: 9, 11, 19, 24. **4.** 464: rev. 7. **18** [kan]. 464: 2. **23.** 8: rev. 15. **50.** 463: 6, 7. **3000.** 3: 4.

PROPER NAMES.

m U-ak-sa-tar, 464: rev. 6.
alu U-a-si, 2: 9, 14.
alu U-e-si, 3: rev. 6.
m Abû-ul-i-di, 462: 4.
m A-bit-šar-uṣur, 5: 2.
mâtu U-ka-a-a, 2: 10; 3: rev. 1.
mâtu Akkad-a-a, 2: 5.
mâtu Akkad (ki), 7: 6.
m Up-pi-te, 464: 12.
alu A-ra-ak-di, 1: 20, rev. 9.
m alu Arba-ilu-a-a, 1: 5, 12.

alu Ur-ia-ku, 464: 13.
alu Arrapḫa, 1: 11, rev. 26.
alu Ur-zu-ḫi-na, 1: 8, 18, 23, rev. 8, 31.
alu Ar-zu-ḫi-na, 1: rev. 5.
amêlu Aš-da-a-a-ti, 6: rev. 11.
m Išdi-ḫarrâni, 1: 7, 10.
m Aš-pa-ba-ra, 464: 9.
E-šarra(ki), 458: 3.
Ašur, 458: 8; 459: 4.
mâtu Aššur(ki), 2: rev. 8; 458: 6.
alu Aššur (LIB ALI), 458: 5.
m Ašur-Dûr-pa-ni-[a], 462: 2.
m Ašur-ri-ṣu-a, 3: 2.
m Ištar-šum-er-eš, 6: 2.
amêlu I-tu-'-a-a, 463: 7.

ilu Bêl, 8: 7.
ilu Bêltu, 458: 8; 459: 4.
m ilu Bêltu-kab-din(?), 6: rev. 8.
mâtu Ba-bi-ti, 1: rev. 18.
m Bab-ba-ni, 7: 4.
mâtu Bar-ḫal-ṣa, 11: 4.

m Gil-ṣa-na, 2: 1.

alu Dûr-ta-li-ti, 1: 15, rev. 1.
alu Dûr-fatânâ pl.-te, 1: rev. 13.
[alu] Dûr-Šar-ukîn, 8: rev. 3.

alu Ḫal-ṣu, 463:4.
alu Ḫa-ri-pa, 464: 9.

m Ṭâbu-ṣil-Ešarra, 458: 2; 459: 2.

mâtu Kal-da-a-a, 462: 5.
amêlu Kal-da-a-a, 5: 5.
alu Kâr-mŠar-ukîn, 464: 3, rev. 9.

m Lu-tu-u, 464: 8.

nâru ME, 3: 8.
mâtu Ma-ṣa-mu, 1: 13.
alu Mu-ṣa-ṣir, 2: rev. 1; 3: 7.
ilu Marduk, 6: 4; 8: 5.
alu Mu-ti-an-ni, 11: 6.

---

ilu Nabû, 6: 4; 8: 5, 7.
m ilu Nabû-er-eš, 5: 4.
m ilu Nabû-lal-an-ni, 464: rev. 4.
m ilu Nabû-šum-iddina, 8: 2.
ilu Nergal, 8: 7.

---

m Si-e-ti-ni, 3: 6, 10.
alu Sa-ba-ḫa-ni, 463: 8.
m Su-na-a, 3: 12.

---

amêlu Ḳur-ra-a-a, 463: 6.

---

m Ra-ma........i, 464: rev. 10.

---

m Šam-ḫu-ilu Ša-maš, 4: 2.
m Šamaš-emur-an-ni, 463: 2.
m Šamaš-bêl-uṣur, 1: 2.
m Šar........7: 2.

---

alu Ta-ga-la-gi, 1: 16.

VITA.

I, George Ricker Berry, was born in West Sumner, Maine, on the 15th of October, 1865. I prepared for college at Hebron Academy. I received the degree of A.B. from Colby University in 1885. Part of the following year was spent in teaching. During the years 1886-1889, I studied at Newton Theological Institution, pursuing the usual Theological course, but giving special attention to the Semitic Languages under Professors O. S. Stearns and C. R. Brown. From 1892 to 1895 I was a Graduate student at The University of Chicago, devoting myself especially to Assyrian under Professor Robert Francis Harper. I have also pursued the study of the other Semitic Languages under President William R. Harper, Professor Emil G. Hirsch, and others.

www.ingramcontent.com/pod-product-compliance
Lightning Source LLC
Chambersburg PA
CBHW032118080426
42733CB00008B/981
9783337019105